Acknowledgements

This book was realized with the help and support of my family, in particular my wife Pamela, my daughters Caitlin and Meghan, and my grand-daughters Saoirse and Rhea. Caitlin, an accomplished editor, guided me through the entire process, ensuring that my first publication reached an acceptable professional level. My family has been both inspirational and patient with me during this shared labor of love. Without their attentiveness to detail, I would not have been able to produce this book, of which I am extremely proud.

Special recognition has to go to my granddaughter, Saoirse. She was the inspirational factor in rediscovering my forgotten talent for drawing. Thank you, Saoirse!

Another note of recognition goes to the late U.S. Representative and activist John Lewis. "When you see something that is not right, not fair, not just, say something! Do something! . . . Get in trouble, good trouble! Necessary trouble!" Inspired by the courage of John Lewis, I decided that my drawings needed to be unleashed upon the public. Whether you like them or not, they are my interpretation of the abysmal and dysfunctional (now former) president and his administration.

Thank you for taking the time and interest in *Welcome to the Swamp*. I hope you have a few laughs along the way.

—SD (TD)

STANDARD DOYLE PUBLICATIONS

© 2021 Swampy Don

Cover design © Tim Doyle
Cover and interior illustrations © Tim Doyle

ISBN 978-1-7365528-0-3

Printed and bound in the United States
by Bookmobile Craft Digital

Swampy Don Presents

WELCOME TO THE SWAMP

An Illustrated Journey into the Deplorable World of Donald J. Trump

"D.C. Swamp Has Gotten Swampier Under Trump"

UPI

"22 Million Americans Support Nazis"

The INDEPENDENT

"Jeanine Pirro Rips William Barr as Swamp Creature"

The Washington Times

"Trump Throws Tantrum; No One Came to His Party"

VANITY FAIR

"Barr Pledged to Protect the Justice Department; He's Destroying It Instead"

"Trump to Send More Than 100 Federal Agents to Portland"

"Pentagon Chief Rejects Trump's Threat to Use Military to Quell Unrest"

"Roger Stone's Commutation . . . Indefensible"

"What the Hell Is Happening with Stephen Miller's Hair?"

"Republicans Bowing to
'Demagogue' Trump
out of Fear"

The INDEPENDENT

"Nothing Can Justify the Attack on Portland"

"Trump Wants to Destroy the USPS"

"I understand the administration is planning on making changes to the postal system."

"How the 'Stolen Election' Myth Will Swallow the GOP"

The Washington Post

"Trump's New Favorite COVID Doctor Believes in Alien DNA, Demon Sperm, and Hydroxychloroquine"

"Trump Called Kamala Harris 'NASTY'—Is It Because She Grills Powerful Men?"

"How Many Trump Advisers
Have Been Criminally Charged?"

"Trump Uses White House as Campaign Backdrop"

"Trump and Barr Discard Law, Morality and Honor"

"Why White Evangelicals See Trump as Their Savior"

"Fascism will come to America
wrapped in a flag and carrying a cross" *

T Daye 2020

*attributed to Sinclair Lewis

"Trump Golfs Instead of Reaching out to Fallen Soldiers' Families"

"Trump Poached Art from Ambassador's Home in Paris"

"Russia's Navalny in Coma, Allegedly Poisoned by Toxic Tea"

"Vladi, the election isn't going as planned!"

"Well Donald, perhaps you should invite your opponent over for a nice cup of tea."

"Trump Took $70,000 in Tax Deductions for Hair Care"

The New York Times

"Dexamethasone: Side Effect of Drug Includes Grandiose Illusions"

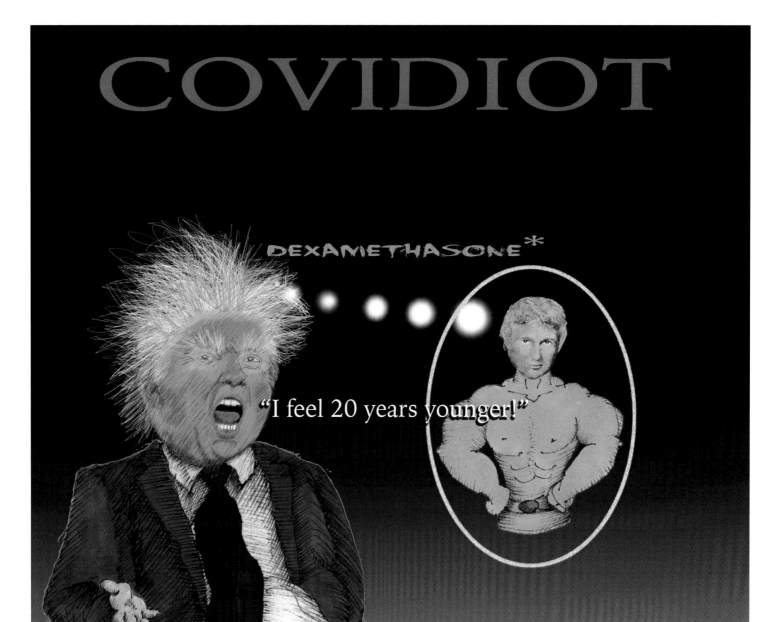

"Mitch McConnell: The Man Who Sold America"

"Trump Tries to Steamroll Biden into Chaotic Clash"

"Debating with Trump is like trying to play chess with a pigeon.
No matter how good you are at chess, the pigeon just knocks
over all of the pieces, shits on the board, and struts around like it won."

Anonymous

"Mike Pence Admits He Was Oblivious . . ."

"Donald Trump's Malignant Narcissism Is Toxic"

"He is a self-made man who worships his creator."

John Bright

"Like the Deranged King George III, the QAnon Lionheart Has Lost America"

"Kushner Bragged that Trump Was Taking the Country 'Back from the Doctors'"

PRIVILEGED
COMPLICIT
IGNORANT
ARROGANT
"Trump's in charge, not the doctors."
Jared Kushner
COVID RESPONSE for RED STATES ONLY
T Doyle 2020

"Putin-Trump Bromance"

Newsweek

"Vladi, your plan didn't work!
Is your guesthouse still available?"

T Doyle 2020

"Sorry, Donald. No can do. I have my self-respect."

"Fearing Jail, Trump Will Not Leave Office Quietly"

YOU'RE FIRED
THIS IS MY SHOW AND I'M NOT LEAVING, NO MATTER WHAT!
T Doyle 2020

"Trump's Tantrum Over Loss Could Smash GOP"

"Whatever It Is, It's Probably Not Hair Dye"

The New York Times

"Rudy, I think there may be a problem; your brains are leaking out."

"Geraldo Rivera Has Had Enough of 'Entitled Frat Boy' Trump"

"Knock it off, entitled frat boy!"
MAKE AMERICA GREAT AGAIN
T Doyle 2020

"They Didn't Drink the Bleach, but They're Still Drinking the Kool-Aid"

The New York Times

"What the Hell Are We Supposed to Do Now?"

politicus®

"Trump Accuses Democrats of Cheating? What Goes Around Comes Around"

"Why Trump Fears Leaving
the White House"

Bloomberg

"Trump Told Them to Fight"

"Capitol Riots: Did Trump's Words Incite Violence?"

"Trump Prepares Pardon Wave for Final Hour"

The New York Times

"'Coward': MAGA Internet Turns on Trump"

POLITICO

"Trump and His Kids Could Go to Prison
as DA Confirms Criminal Bank Fraud Investigation"

politicus.

The Donald J. Trump
Clown Show
Proudly Presents
the
Cast of Misfits

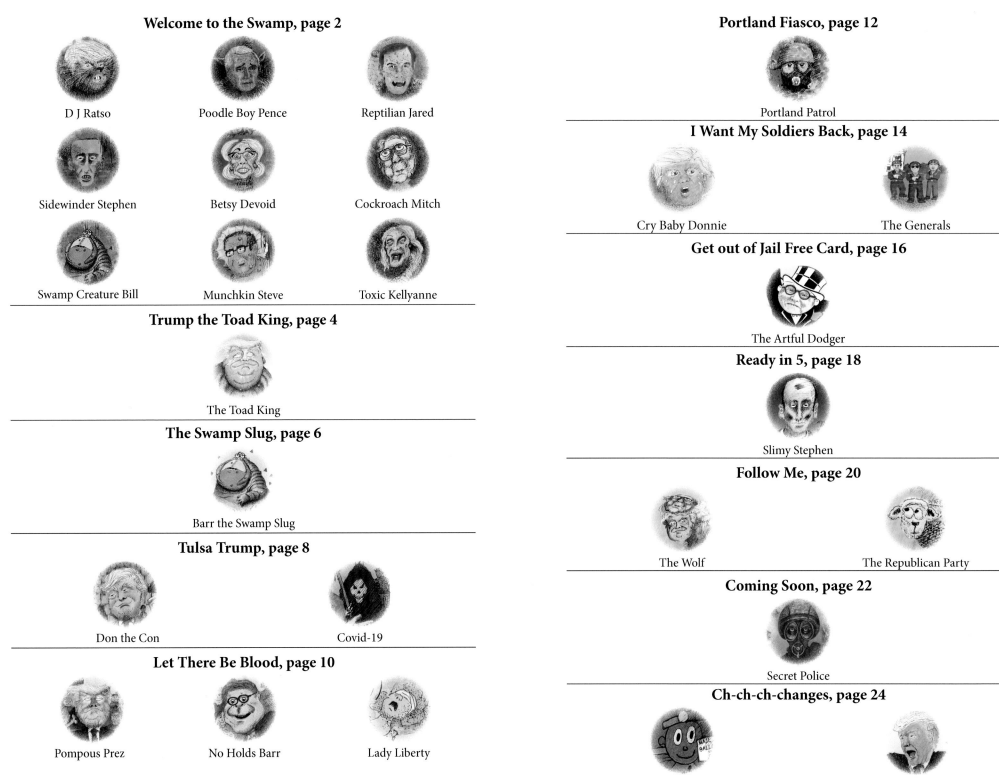

Welcome to the Swamp, page 2

D J Ratso

Poodle Boy Pence

Reptilian Jared

Sidewinder Stephen

Betsy Devoid

Cockroach Mitch

Swamp Creature Bill

Munchkin Steve

Toxic Kellyanne

Trump the Toad King, page 4

The Toad King

The Swamp Slug, page 6

Barr the Swamp Slug

Tulsa Trump, page 8

Don the Con

Covid-19

Let There Be Blood, page 10

Pompous Prez

No Holds Barr

Lady Liberty

Portland Fiasco, page 12

Portland Patrol

I Want My Soldiers Back, page 14

Cry Baby Donnie

The Generals

Get out of Jail Free Card, page 16

The Artful Dodger

Ready in 5, page 18

Slimy Stephen

Follow Me, page 20

The Wolf

The Republican Party

Coming Soon, page 22

Secret Police

Ch-ch-ch-changes, page 24

USPS Zippy

Dangerous Don

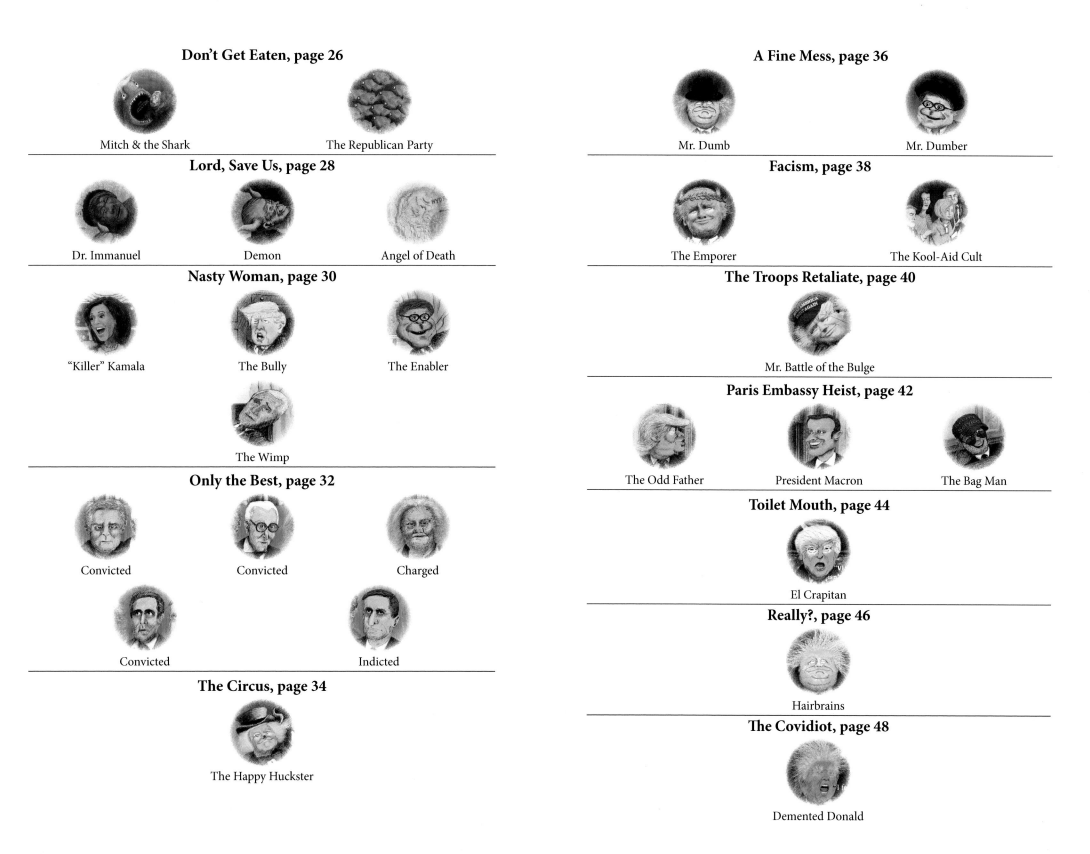

Don't Get Eaten, page 26

Mitch & the Shark

The Republican Party

Lord, Save Us, page 28

Dr. Immanuel

Demon

Angel of Death

Nasty Woman, page 30

"Killer" Kamala

The Bully

The Enabler

The Wimp

Only the Best, page 32

Convicted

Convicted

Charged

Convicted

Indicted

The Circus, page 34

The Happy Huckster

A Fine Mess, page 36

Mr. Dumb

Mr. Dumber

Facism, page 38

The Emporer

The Kool-Aid Cult

The Troops Retaliate, page 40

Mr. Battle of the Bulge

Paris Embassy Heist, page 42

The Odd Father

President Macron

The Bag Man

Toilet Mouth, page 44

El Crapitan

Really?, page 46

Hairbrains

The Covidiot, page 48

Demented Donald

Wicked, page 50

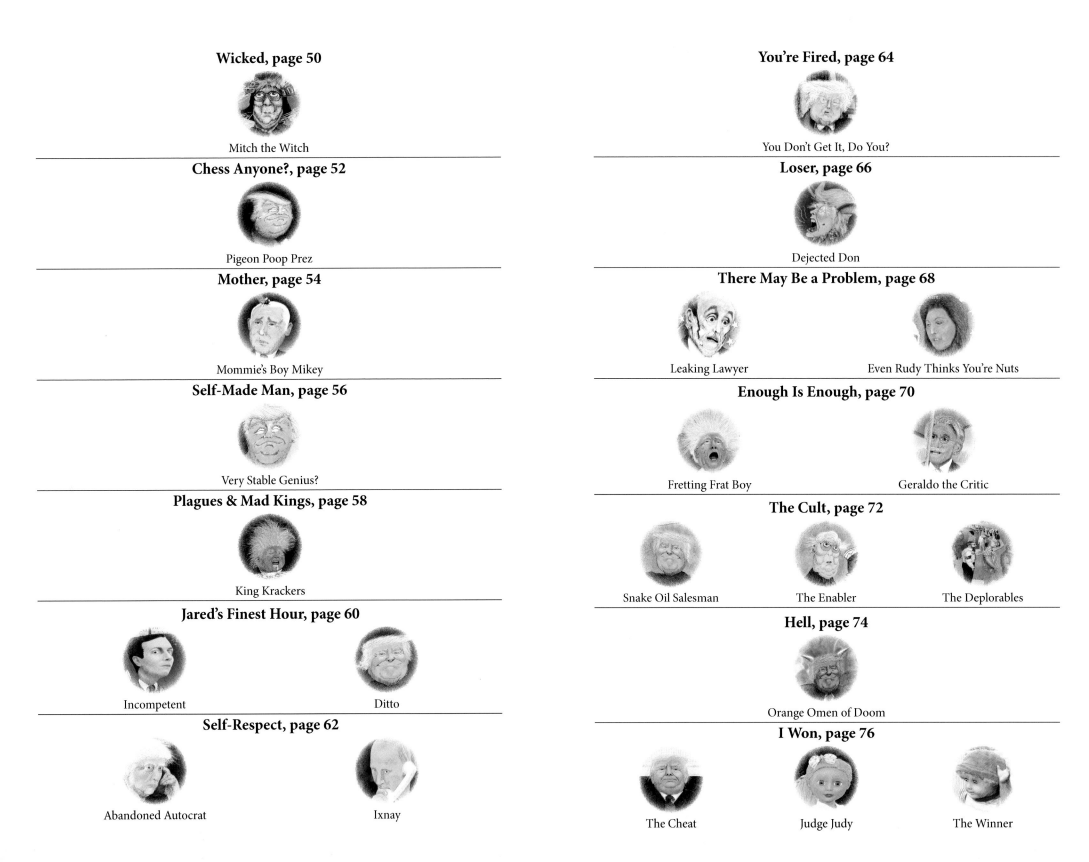

Mitch the Witch

Chess Anyone?, page 52

Pigeon Poop Prez

Mother, page 54

Mommie's Boy Mikey

Self-Made Man, page 56

Very Stable Genius?

Plagues & Mad Kings, page 58

King Krackers

Jared's Finest Hour, page 60

Incompetent   Ditto

Self-Respect, page 62

Abandoned Autocrat   Ixnay

You're Fired, page 64

You Don't Get It, Do You?

Loser, page 66

Dejected Don

There May Be a Problem, page 68

Leaking Lawyer   Even Rudy Thinks You're Nuts

Enough Is Enough, page 70

Fretting Frat Boy   Geraldo the Critic

The Cult, page 72

Snake Oil Salesman   The Enabler   The Deplorables

Hell, page 74

Orange Omen of Doom

I Won, page 76

The Cheat   Judge Judy   The Winner

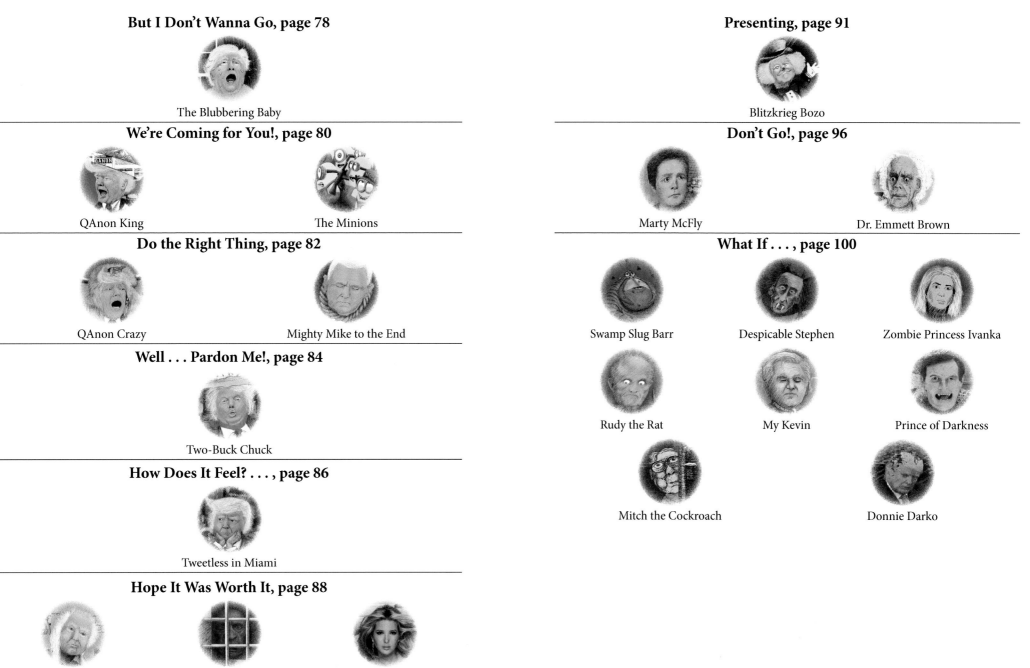

"We Were Warned"

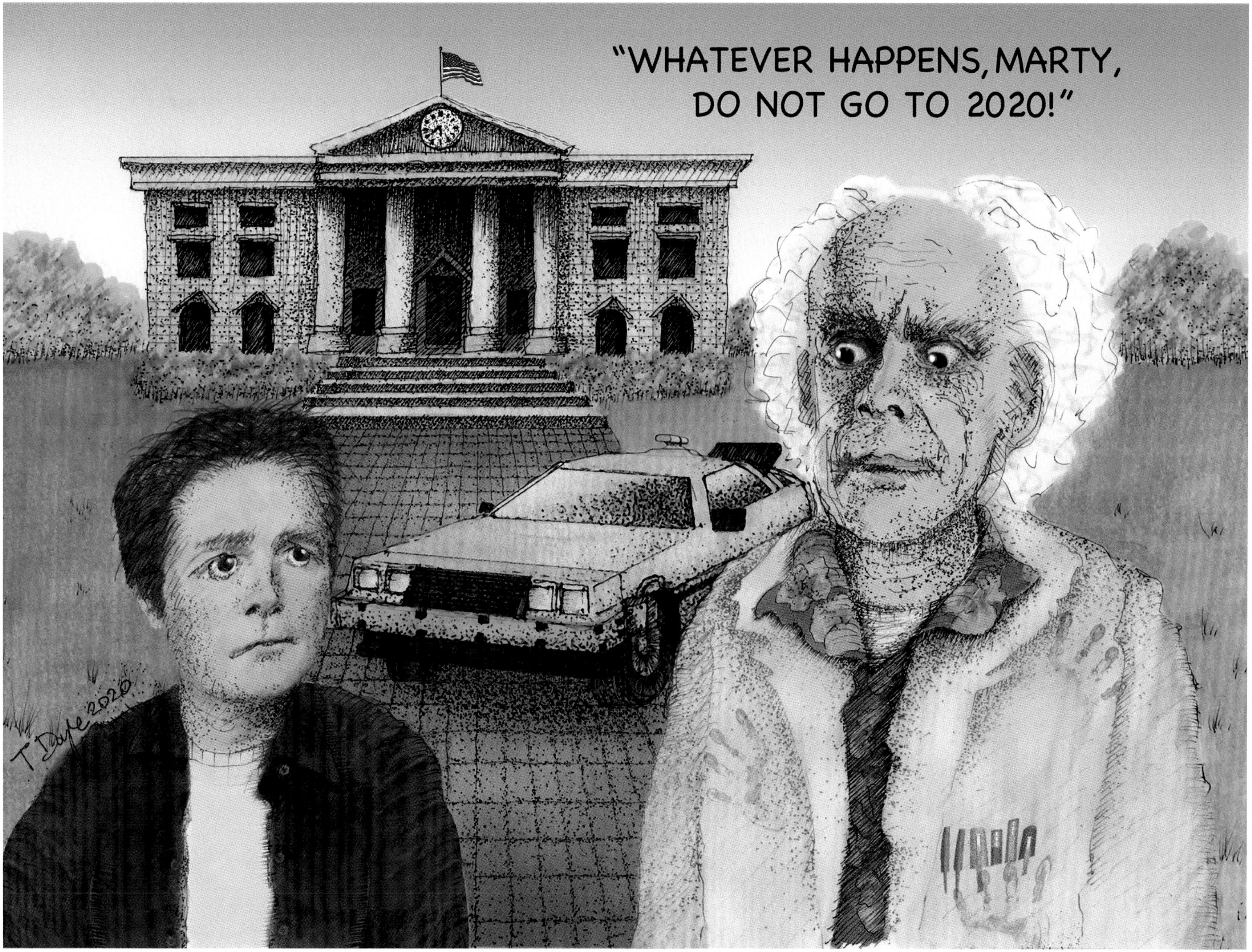
"WHATEVER HAPPENS, MARTY,
DO NOT GO TO 2020!"
T Daye 2020

Reference:
The use of a source of information
in order to ascertain something
"Democracy Dies in Darkness"
The Washington Post
Dr. Fauci
T Doyle 2021

References

2   D.C. Swamp Has Gotten Swampier / *UPI*
By Sara Swann, June 19, 2020

4   Support of Nazis / *The Independent UK*
By Mary Oppenheim, Aug 22, 2017

6   Jeanine Pirro Rips William Barr as Swamp Creature /
Washington Times
By Cheryl K Chumley, Dec 7, 2020

8   Trump's Tulsa Tantrum / *Vanity Fair*
By Charlotte Klein, June 22, 2020

10   Destruction of Justice / *USA Today*
By Editorial Board, Feb 26, 2020

12   More Troops / *FOX News*
By Barnini Chakraborty, July 27, 2020

14   Military says NO! / *NPR*
By David Welna, June 3, 2020

16   Roger Stone's Commutation / *National Review*
By The Editors, July 12, 2020

18   Stephen Miller's Hair / *Esquire*
By Jonathan Evans, Dec 17, 2020

20   Republicans Lead by Trump / *The Independent UK*
By Harriet Alexander, Dec 14, 2020

22   Nothing Can Justify the Attack / *The Atlantic*
By Quinta Jurecic and Benjamin Wittes, July 21, 2020

24   Destruction of Postal System / *The Guardian*
By Nathan Robinson, Aug 17, 2020

26   Swallow the GOP / *The Washington Post*
By Opinion, Dec 7, 2020

28   Demon Sperm / *The Daily Beast*
By Will Sommer, July 28, 2020

30   Nasty Woman / *The Guardian*
By Poppy Noor, Aug 12, 2020

32   Trump Advisors Charged / *USA Today*
By Kevin Johnson, Aug 21, 2020

34   White House as Backdrop / *The Hill*
By Cate Martel, Aug 26, 2020

36   Trump and Barr Discard Law / *Bloomberg*
Timothy L O'Brien, June 21, 2020

38   Facism and the Savior / *The Guardian*
By Adam Gabbatt, Jan 11, 2020

40   Trump Golfs Instead of Respecting Fallen Soldiers /
The American Independent
By Eric Boehlert, Oct 19, 2017

42   Paris Art Theft / *Political Wire*
By Taegan Goddard, Sept 6, 2020

44   Toxic Tea / *Associated Press*
By Daria Litvinova, Aug 20,2020

46    $70,000 for Hair Care / *NY Times*
By James B Stewart, Oct 6, 2020

48   Dexamethasone / *Newsweek*
By Kashmira Gander, Oct 5, 2020

50   The Man Who Sold America / *Rolling Stone*
By Bob Moser, Sept 17, 2019

52   First Presidential Debate / *The Guardian*
By Joan E Greve, Sept 30, 2020

54   Pence Was Oblivious / *HUFFPOST*
By Lee Moran, Oct 13, 2020

56   Malignant Narcissism / *USA Today*
By John Gartner, May 4, 2017

58   The Madness of King Trump / *The Guardian*
By Ian Martin, Nov 18, 2020

60   Jared's Finest Hour / *CNN*
By Michael Warren, Jamie Gangel, and Elizabeth Stuart,
Oct 28, 2020

62   Putin-Trump Bromance / *Newsweek*
By Damien Sharkov, July 16, 2018

64   Trump Will Not Leave / *Salon*
By Bill Blum, July 16, 2020

66   Trump Tantrum Over Loss / *The Daily Beast*
By Sam Brodley and Hunter Woodal, Nov 30, 2020

68   Whatever It Is . . . / *NY Times*
By Jonah Engel Bromwich, Nov 19, 2020

70   Entitled Frat Boy / *US News*
By Jeremy Blum, Dec 27, 2020

72   They Didn't Drink the Bleach / *NY Times*
By Frank Bruni, April 29, 2020

74   What The Hell Are We Supposed to do Now? / *Politicus*
By Geraldo Rivera, Dec 23, 2020

76   Trump Accuses Democrats / *Washington Examiner*
By Byron York, Nov 8, 2020

78   Why Trump Fears Leaving White House / *Bloomberg*
By Timothy L O'Brien, Nov 11, 2020

80   Trump Summoned Supporters to "Wild" Protest / *Reuters*
By Steve Holland, Jeff Mason, and Jonathan Landy,
Jan 6, 2021

82   Capitol Riots: Trump Incites Violence / *BBC News*
By Sam Cabral, Jan 13, 2021

84   Trump Prepares Pardon Wave for Final Hours / *NY Times*
By Maggie Haberman, Kenneth P. Vogel, and Dana
Rubenstein, Jan 18, 2021

86   Donald Trump's Most Ardent Online Fans Have Finally
Turned on Him / *Politico*
by Tina Nguyen, Jan 8, 2021

88   Trump & Kids Could Go to Prison / *Politicus*
By Jason Easley, Aug 3, 2020